Being Sober

50 Things To Do Instead Of Getting F***ED Up

Grandma Kickass

Table Of Contents

Introduction — 3

Chapter 1 – How It All Begins — 4

Chapter 2 – Clever Things You Can Do At Home…Instead of Getting F***ed Up — 7

Chapter 3 – Are You Bored At Work? Read This! — 13

Chapter 4 – Having Fun Socializing…Without Getting F***ed Up — 16

Chapter 5 – Weird Things People Do To Be Entertained — 19

Conclusion — 22

The Grandma Kickass Collection: — 23

Copyright 2014 by <u>Globalized Healing, LLC</u> - All rights reserved.

Introduction

Let's face it! One of the worst feelings is being bored and one of the main reasons people use drugs or alcohol is because they're bored. More specifically they're bored with situations they are currently involved in and they want to experience something exciting and new. They want something new to fill time and fill the gap where boredom once existed.

Naturally, people like to feel useful and productive – and when people are stuck in a place of boredom they turn to... Drugs & alcohol. Therefore this book was with one key purpose: To give you a s**t-load of fun, creative things to do to entertain the mind and fill your time... So you will NEVER be bored again!

Your emotions are about to go on a roller-coaster ride as you begin seeing yourself participating in what you are about to read.

Hold on, have fun and enjoy the ride!

Chapter 1 – How It All Begins

Boredom is a state of mind. A choice... A torture. It is a trigger that pushes people into doing things that they know they shouldn't be, such as drinking too much alcohol, taking drugs and engaging in casual sex. These are all acts of instant gratification, which can, later on, turn into addiction. Boredom often causes people to act before even thinking, which often leads to trouble and grave consequences.

But how can we beat boredom? It's part of our everyday lives. But it doesn't have to be. There are a multitude of reasons why we should strive to eliminate it from our lives. The following list might make you examine your free time twice next time you feel like just lounging on your couch with nothing to do.

- Left unchecked, boredom stands poised to take over your life.
- Boredom has been proven to be detrimental to your health.
- Boredom can overtake your social life.
- As odd as it seems, boredom can become a bad habit. This can prevent you from ever trying new things and expanding your horizons.
- Boredom can cause problems between family members, friends, and even worse, the authorities.
- Boredom is generally stressful and depressing, leading to feelings of being unwanted and worthless.
- Boredom often leads you to losing your patience.
- Boredom can lead you to losing your job.
- Boredom can be a threat and beat the life out of you.

Boredom is a case by case basis... Some people get bored while being ordered around, feeling like they have no mind of their own. Other people get bored when doing repetitive tasks... And yet others get bored because they simply have nothing to do.

One of the best pieces of advice that can be offered on how to stave off boredom is to exert effort in everything you do, and be determined every day to live life to the fullest. We only have so much time to live – don't waste a single day languishing, bored. Try to make each day a fulfilling one. Here are some other helpful tips that can help keep you occupied and out of trouble.

- Stay away from activities and people with negative vibes.
- Find things in your life to improve upon... Nobody is perfect.
- Always keep a positive mindset and outlook on life.
- Learn to explore and try new things with new friends. Get out of your comfort zone, have fun! But always be mindful of your limits. Never do anything you feel is wrong.
- Keep looking forward, finding new challenges and activities in your daily life.
- Don't pull your punches, go all out and give everything you do your very best shot. Always. Keep. Challenging. Yourself. Staying in one place with something will inevitably lead back to boredom. Achieving more than you expected you could brings a sense of satisfaction and fulfillment not found elsewhere in life. Challenging yourself never hurts.

Now is time to take charge and stop boredom from taking over your life. There is no need to wait for someone to pull you out of your misery – go do it yourself! You are the only one stopping you. Remember – Boredom is just a choice. There are so many things to do and experience with your life – so many that it would take ten lifetimes with which to do them all. So why would you choose to sit around all day? Why would you ever choose to be bored?

The next few chapters of this book are to give you some ideas on exactly what to do to begin your journey to never being bored again. Nothing too challenging – they are simple and easy, yet almost guaranteed to beat the boredom right out of you.

Chapter 2 – Clever Things You Can Do At Home…Instead of Getting F***ed Up

Living life to the fullest… Isn't this everyone's goal? Living a life in boredom is probably the most horrific torture for the human mind – it's one of the most basic psychological elements of putting people in prison. Having said that, why would you ever make yourself a prisoner in your own home? Answer? You don't have to. Remember – boredom is a choice.

Ask yourself, how far can you go? Can you really just sit and watch as the day goes by with nothing to do? How would you feel sleeping all day while others are out socializing? Would you really be satisfied if you just stared at the four walls of your bedroom? If the answer is yes, well, then you are definitely missing out. If that's not what you want out of your life, then all you have to do is get out of be and go out into the world to give the day a fighting chance.

Try some of these suggestions:

1. Your house, your home, is a great place to start. Try cleaning your room. Really, REALLY cleaning your room. Doing this will keep you busy. Maybe it's time for you to redecorate and give your room a total transformation. You can change your room's wallpaper into something more modern. Maybe you even repaint the walls. Change your bed sheets and covers, make sure that the color you choose compliment the color of the walls and carpet. Add furniture and wall frames to give life to your room. And then, to top it all off, invite your friends for a sleepover to show off your newly transformed room.

2. Exert effort in organizing the clothes in your closet. Check your entire wardrobe to see if there are clothes you don't wear anymore. You probably have dozens of items you might want to get rid of by now. You may want to donate it to charity. Clear some space for new things.

3. Instead of lying in bed all day, make yourself productive and do your laundry. You have to learn how to wash your own clothes. Do not rely on others to do it for you. Learning how to live independently includes doing your own laundry.

4. Cooking can always keep you out of boredom's reach. Cooking is not just for chefs. Time to bring out your reliable, good old cook book and start trying new recipes. Or you can always create your own and experiment. Forget take - outs. Having the same food every... single... day... is completely boring. Nobody wants that.

5. Bake your favorite cake. Or you can try to be bolder and bake a complicated cake recipe. Have your family try your latest cake creation. Invite your friends over to test your culinary creations.

6. Get creative with your food. Try building a tower sandwich like old Saturday morning cartoons. Try some new cuisine, if you like Mexican, cook some Italian dishes.

7. Instead of ordering delivery, make your own pizza. Add your favorite flavors and toppings, such as pepperoni, 4 cheese, ham and cheese, mushrooms, olives, and bacon.

8. Experiment with making your own homemade ice cream. Research for the instructions and ingredients from the internet. You might want to serve ice cream for the entire family.

9. Organizing your cabinet drawers another way of keeping yourself busy. There are probably a lot of things which need reorganizing in your drawers. Get rid of things that are no longer needed to clear some space for new stuff.

10. Not all old habits are bad – playing video games can certainly be entertaining, but be careful that it doesn't become addicting. Limit your play time and try to engage in more productive tasks.

11. Surfing the web is a surefire way to cure boredom. Get online, make some friends, research topics that interest you but you've never had time to study. You might even try building your own website.

12. Interact online by chatting with your social network friends. It's good to just gossip once in a while. Aside from chatting online, there are many other things to do when you log-in to Facebook, Twitter or Instagram. You can read, like, and comment on your friends' statuses, upload your latest pictures, and engage in conversation with your latest love interest. You can do this all day.

13. Read your favorite novel or flip through the pages of your favorite magazine. You probably wouldn't even notice how many hours have passed before you finish reading the entire book. Reading adds to your knowledge, and at the same time keeps you occupied.

14. Pamper yourself e when at home. Take long baths and showers. Fix and style your hair. Paint your nails. Try different kinds of makeup. Bring out your inner Fashionista by trying out the latest looks and styles. Looking good will make you feel good.

15. If you have a pet, give him a bath. Play with them or try to teach them some new tricks. You may also bring your pet to veterinarian for a regular checkup. Alternatively you may bring them to a pet grooming store to pamper them.

16. If living with someone, be sure to help out with household chores, such as washing the dishes, cleaning the table, watering the plants and mowing the lawn. It's good to be domesticated once in a while.

17. Watch a re-run of your favorite TV series. Drool over your favorite actors and actresses.

18. Check your fridge and see if you're in need of supplies. You might be out of butter, milk or eggs. List the things you needed to buy from the grocery.

19. Try new things like planting your own garden. This is one of the most rewarding tasks. Creating things and watching living things grow is incredibly enjoyable. This is something you can be proud of someday.

20. Make a short errand to the nearest grocery store and do some shopping. Buy your favorite foods, such as chocolates, some chips, juices, milk, and vegetables. Shopping gets you out of the house for a while.

21. Invite friends over for dinner. It's always nice to have friends over, plus, you could show off your cooking

skills. Friends can always cheer you up.

22. Watching movies can always relax your mind. You might try having a movie marathon with family members or inviting friends over to watch with you. While watching, you can munch on popcorn or your favorite chips.

23. Call your friends and see if they would like to go to the mall during the day or clubbing at night. There might be a concert of your favorite group to go to. Getting out of the house once in a while is healthy. Socializing with others can boost your self confidence. Don't confine yourself at home all the time. Don't worry about being left out – just go out and do it.

24. Plan a trip, either with family or with friends. A vacation allows you to unwind and relax, especially if you are stressed out from work. Check the area out online beforehand for places you might like to go visit. Travelling to a new environment is exciting and motivating – nobody is bored on vacation.

25. One of the best ways to deal with boredom at home is to interact with your family. You might have neglected them for a very long time and it might be one of the reasons why you feel so bored at home. It always feels good to talk to your parents, brothers, or sisters. Ask them how their day went. A simple "Hi" from you can mean the world to them. Though you live in the same house, you might even be surprised to realize that you miss them too. Try surprising them by cooking dinner or treating them to a night out.

There is always something to do when boredom strikes at home. Just do something that would keep your mind and body busy. The most important thing to remember is to always have fun and allowing yourself to relax sometimes.

Chapter 3 – Are You Bored At Work? Read This!

Being in the office eight hours a day can bore you to tears. Not all jobs are as exciting as the jobs of actors and actresses. Not all jobs give you the privilege to travel most of the time. An ordinary workplace can be very busy during the day, or there might be days with nothing to accomplish at all. Things might be a little slow or there might be a lot going on. Doesn't matter, work is usually pretty boring. Doing the same routine every day will only serve to make you grumpy.

There might be times you will find yourself questioning, is staying at this job still worth it? Are you still growing in the company? How can you survive another day at work? Will resignation end your boredom? These are probably some of the questions playing in your head.

Here are some of the things to do that can cure boredom at your workplace:

1. If you are done with your work and you have nothing else to do, ask one of your colleagues if they need help on what they're doing. It is better to have something to do than doing nothing at all. Helping coworkers also allows you to interact and talk to them. Having no one to talk to can drive you crazy. It is always better to make yourself productive.

2. Tidy up your workspace if you are done with your task. Cleaning will keep you busy. Call maintenance to empty your trash.

3. Organize your files. Label them so it won't be difficult for you to find them when your boss asks for it. Get rid of some files that are no longer needed, or have someone help you to transfer them in the storage place where old files are kept.

4. Clear your desk. Remove all clutter from your desk, such as pens, folders, papers and paper clips. Have a pen holder where you can place your pens and pencils or a paper clip holder. It is better to work when your desk is clean.

5. If you have a lot to accomplish in a day, listen to music. Listen to your favorite songs while working. Music can ease tension and minimize boredom.

6. Always take your breaks, especially if the volume of work is killing you. Eat healthy, rounded snacks such as: bananas, pistachios, or grapes. Never skip lunch. Skipping lunch will only make your mood worse.

7. Bring your favorite book. You can read during your free time.

8. During your free time, check all the files on your computer. Delete or place older files in your archive.

9. During your free time, check your inbox. Read all of your new messages. Delete messages that are no longer needed. Clear some space for incoming new ones. Filter your messages so it would be easier to search for a topic when necessary.

10. Check your work calendar. You can start working on new projects during your free time. It would keep your mind working.

11. Socialize with your colleagues after office hours. Some may opt to have a drink at the nearest bar. Socializing can ease stress and boredom.

12. If your work is done for the day and you still have a lot of free time before your shift ends, take time to evaluate your performance. Reevaluate your goals. If you feel like your career is not going anywhere, consider having a chat with your boss. Discuss your options. It I always good to know where you stand in the company. If you feel like your career is reaching a dead end, it might be time for you to consider other possibilities.

13. Plan a vacation. This is the best thing to do when boredom strikes you at your workplace. Take a few days off from work. Going on a trip will clear and relax your mind. Always find the time to reenergize yourself.

These are some of the things that can help you get through a rough day at work. One of the keys to curing boredom at work is to keep yourself busy. Another key is to evaluate your goals. You can never be satisfied if you feel your career is not going anywhere.

Chapter 4 – Having Fun Socializing...
Without Getting F***ed Up

Socializing is not always fun. Doing the same routine with friends can be boring too. Dining in the same restaurant every day, gossiping about the same person, watching the same type of movies, and wearing the same type of clothes can be very tiring to the point it gets too boring.

Why not try new things? Why don't you try doing things you don't normally do? These things can make your life more interesting.

Here are some of the things you might want to try:

1. Help in community work. This would be a new experience for you. Instead of just hanging out with your friends, why don't you persuade them to do something more productive that can contribute to the community? Your group may opt to do volunteer work, such as helping in feeding the poor, teaching children to read, and visiting sick people in government hospitals.

2. You and your friends can learn different skills and discover new hobbies. Your group can join different clubs, such as cooking clubs, writing clubs, dance clubs, drama clubs, and swimming clubs. This is something you and your group will look forward to. Joining different clubs will also mean meeting new friends.

3. Throw a party at your home. Instead of attending parties, why don't you be the host of your own party?

Have your friends help you plan this big event. You can invite anyone whom you would like to be there. You get to choose your own theme, the food and the drinks. You can make your party the party of the century.

4. Organize a tournament. Organizing a tournament will truly keep you busy most of the day. You may need help from your friends and sponsors. The tournament may be a volleyball tournament, basketball tournament, or even a tennis match.

5. Donate to charity. This is one of the most rewarding activities. Have your friends and family donate.

6. Join fund raising activities. Joining such activities will increase your social awareness.

7. Try venturing into business. Have your friends or family help you in setting up a juice stand or a hotdog stand. This will keep you out of the boredom zone. You get to interact with people while earning money.

8. Join stage plays. There are some stage plays that will pay you for acting. Acting will give you access to meeting different kinds of people, such as directors and producers. You might even end up having an acting career.

9. Join competitions. Being part of a competition can boost your self confidence. Competitions can be your gateway to travelling and meeting people from different parts of the world. Aside from the prizes, one of the best benefits of joining a competition is that you're given the privilege to live like a star. Your handler will surely take care of you, feed you well,

and train you to be the best. You might even end up signing contracts for sponsors.

10. If you are a student, run for a position in the student body. It will enhance your leadership skills. During your free time, you can focus on how to improve your schooling. If you are a professional, you may opt to run for a position in the government. However, having a position in the government is not that easy. It requires a very big responsibility.

11. Engage yourself in research studies. This will allow you to interact with different people. This also presents the opportunity to gain knowledge of new things.

12. Support projects for a cause. You may also persuade your friends to join your project group. Most of these projects are for the betterment of the environment. An example of a project for a cause is stopping animal cruelty.

Chapter 5 – Weird Things People Do To Be Entertained

There are some simple, funny things that you might end up doing when you are bored. Here's a list of some of those funny things:

1. You might often daydream when you are bored. You daydream about so many things, such as being the president of a multinational company, marrying the person of your dreams, or being a famous actor or actress. Daydreaming exercises the mind.

2. You might end up humming a tune or singing even though your voice sounds like a toad.

3. Taking a self-portrait from time to time, then loading it on Instagram or Facebook. This is a common sign of boredom for many people.

4. You might make your own bucket list. Since you have nothing to do, you list down the things you wanted to do or places where you wanted to go.

5. You might end up solving crossword puzzles.

6. You might dress up like your favorite super hero.

7. You might end up just staring in space.

8. You might end up walking absentmindedly. Then the next minute, you find yourself outside your friend's house, or outside your favorite restaurant.

9. You might end up playing with your food.

10. You end up talking to yourself.

11. You might end up daring yourself to invite your crush over for dinner.

12. You might try different hair styles in a day.

13. You always say yes to whatever your friends are saying, though your mind is not on the subject.

Chapter 6 – Final Words of Wisdom From Grandma Kickass

Always remember that you have a choice to not be bored. There are lists of things to do that can make you productive. Remember these three things when you find yourself dealing with boredom:

- Challenge yourself. Take every challenge that comes your way. Prove to yourself that you can always do better.

- Engage in more physical activities. Exercising is one way to prevent boredom. Exercising releases not only excess body fats, but also excess body stress. Join activities that can help you grow as a person.

- Focus on something that you love doing the most. Do things that interest you. Things that you love doing will never tire nor bore you.

Remember that boredom is not the master of your day to day life. Always choose to end the day being satisfied and content because you have done something interesting. Never waste a minute having idle thoughts.

Conclusion

Thank you for taking the time to read this book.

I hope that it was refreshing for you to hear of the wide array of things you can do when you are beginning to feel boredom set in. Now that you have learned about the nature of boredom and its consequences, what it can do and how it affects life, it is up to you to choose to NEVER be bored again. Go out and fill your free time with fun, creative and interesting things.

Do great things and be proud of yourself. Challenge yourself!

- Grandma K.

The Grandma Kickass Collection:

1.

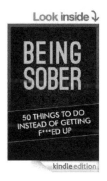

Being Sober: 50 Things To Do Instead Of Getting F***ed Up

2.

Quit Drinking! How To Stop Drinking With Grandma Kickass Grandma's Secret Sauce To Being Sober & Conquering Alcoholism

Being Sober

Printed in Great Britain
by Amazon